KINGFISHER
READERS

level
4

D0676029

Human Body

Anita Ganeri

![Kingfisher logo]

First published 2013 by Kingfisher
an imprint of Macmillan Children's Books
a division of Macmillan Publishers Limited
20 New Wharf Road, London N1 9RR
Basingstoke and Oxford
Associated companies throughout the world
www.panmacmillan.com

Series editor: Polly Goodman
Literacy consultant: Hilary Horton

ISBN: 978-0-7534-3098-9
Copyright © Macmillan Publishers Ltd 2013

9 8 7 6 5 4 3 2 1

1TR/1012/WKT/UG/105MA

A CIP catalogue record for this book is available from the British Library.

Printed in China

Picture credits
The Publisher would like to thank the following for permission to reproduce their material. Every care
has been taken to trace copyright holders. However, if there have been unintentional omissions or failure
to trace copyright holders, we apologize and will, if informed, endeavour to make corrections in any
future edition.
(t = top; b = bottom; c = centre; l = left; r = right):
Cover Corbis/Tim Clayton; Pages 3t Shutterstock/Ralf Juergen Kraft; 3ct Shutterstock/Monkey
Business Images; 3c KF Archive; 3cb Shutterstock/doglikehorse; 3b Corbis/John W. Karapelou,
CMI; 4l KF Archive; 4-5 Shutterstock/Mandy Godbehear; 5t KF Archive; 6t Shutterstock/xpixel; 6b
Shutterstock/Williv; 7 Shutterstock/Ralf Juergen Kraft; 8l KF Archive; 8r KF Archive; 9t KF Archive;
9bl Shutterstock/DenisNata; 9bc Shutterstock/ doglikehorse; 9br Shutterstock/Palmer Kane LLC;
10 KF Archive; 11t Corbis/Creasource; 11b KF Archive; 12 Corbis/John W. Karapelou, CMI; 13 KF
Archive; 14 KF Archive; 15t KF Archive; 15b KF Archive; 16l Alamy/arlyons; 16r KF Archive; 17t
KF Archive; 17b Shutterstock/Xidong Luo; 18 KF Archive; 19 Corbis/Tim Clayton; 20 KF Archive;
21t KF Archive; 21b Corbis/Laura Doss; 22t Corbis/Creasource; 22b KF Archive; 23 KF Archive; 24
KF Archive; 25t KF Archive; 25b Alamy/ableimages; 26t KF Archive; 26b Corbis/Kevin RL Hanson;
27tr Shutterstock/Rob Marmion; 27b Corbis/Randy Faris; 28 Corbis/Janie Airey/Cutural; 29t
Shutterstock/ Monkey Business Images; 29b Corbis/Marnie Burkhart; 31 Corbis/Tim Clayton

Contents

Your body   4

Skeleton   6

Muscles   8

Skin and hair   10

Brain and nerves   12

Seeing and hearing   14

Tasting, smelling and touching   16

Lungs   18

Heart and blood   20

Stomach and digestion   22

Liver and kidneys   24

Birth and growth   26

Illness and health   28

Glossary   30

Index   32

Your body

Your amazing body has thousands of different parts. These work together to help you live and grow. Some parts are on the outside of your body, such as your skin, hair, eyes, ears and limbs. Others are hidden inside you, such as your bones, heart and lungs.

Heart

Lungs

Bones

Cells

Your body is made up of millions and millions of tiny building blocks, called **cells**. Most cells are too small to see except under a microscope. Cells are different shapes and sizes, depending on what job they do. This picture shows red and white blood cells.

Red blood cells

White blood cells

Everyone's body has the same parts, doing the same jobs. But you are the only person exactly like you. Everyone looks different. Some people are tall or short. Some have dark or fair hair. Some have different body shapes and sizes.

Skeleton

Gently squeeze your finger. The hard, knobbly bits you can feel are bones. You have 206 bones inside you, which make up your skeleton. Your skeleton holds your body up. Some bones also protect soft parts of your body. Your skull, for example, protects your brain and your ribs protect your heart and lungs.

Broken bones

Sometimes bones break. Doctors use a special photograph called an X-ray to look at the bone. A bone can mend itself but you might need a plaster cast to help it heal.

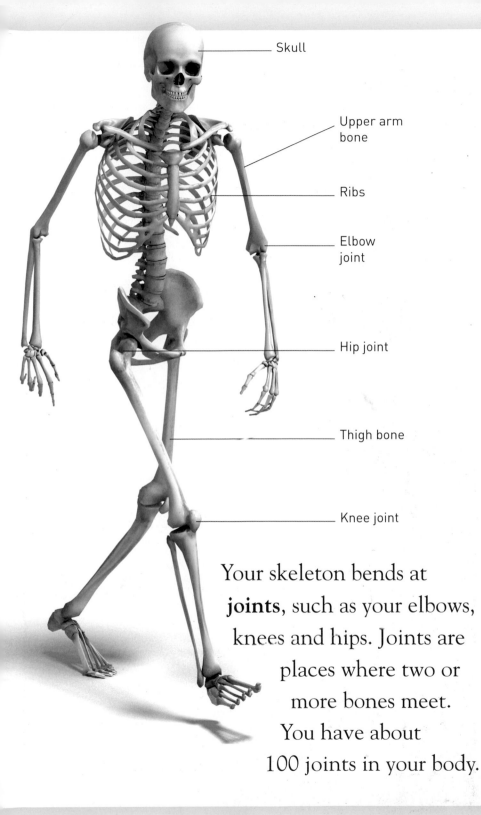

Skull

Upper arm bone

Ribs

Elbow joint

Hip joint

Thigh bone

Knee joint

Your skeleton bends at **joints,** such as your elbows, knees and hips. Joints are places where two or more bones meet. You have about 100 joints in your body.

Muscles

Under your skin, there are hundreds of muscles. Many of them are fastened to your bones by strong straps, called **tendons**. They work with your bones to make you move.

You have about 640 muscles in your body. They make up about a third of your body weight. The biggest muscles are in your bottom and thighs. The smallest muscles are attached to the tiny bones inside your ears.

Playing football uses lots of different muscles.

Muscles of every size are always at work.

8

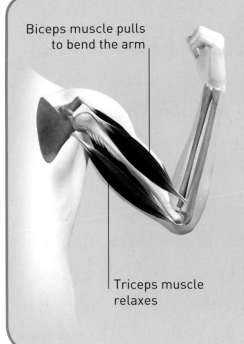

Biceps muscle pulls to bend the arm

Triceps muscle relaxes

Working in pairs

Many muscles work in pairs, such as the biceps and triceps in your arms. To bend your arm, the biceps pulls while the triceps relaxes. To straighten your arm, the triceps pulls while the biceps relaxes.

Not all of your muscles make your bones move. Some muscles make your heart beat and help you to **digest** your food. Tiny muscles in your face pull on your skin to make you smile, blink and pull faces.

Skin and hair

Stretchy skin covers your body. It keeps out **germs** and dirt. Skin is waterproof and helps keep your body at the right temperature. It also helps you to touch and feel things.

Your skin is made up of two layers, called the epidermis and the dermis. The epidermis is the top layer. It is made up of dead skin cells. They are replaced by new skin cells made in the dermis, which push up to the surface.

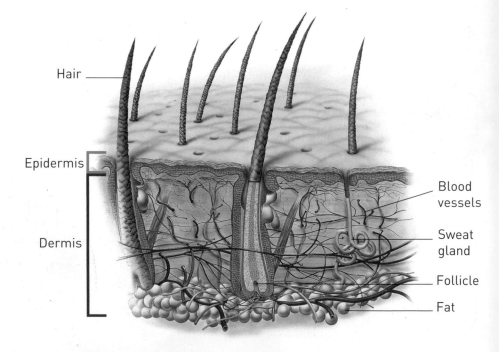

Hair

Epidermis

Dermis

Blood vessels

Sweat gland

Follicle

Fat

Hair grows from pits deep in the dermis, called follicles. Hairs are made up of dead cells. The only living part is inside the follicle.

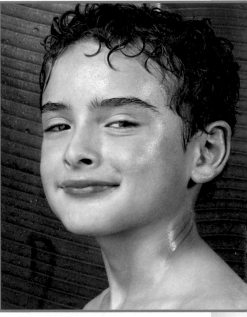

If you get too hot, sweat glands ooze sweat out on to the surface of your skin, which helps cool you down. At the same time, blood vessels in your skin get bigger and let off more heat.

Fingerprints

Can you see tiny patterns on the skin on your fingertips? They help your fingers to grip. They are called fingerprints and everyone's are different.

Brain and nerves

The most important part of your body is your brain. It is hidden underneath your hard skull bones. Your brain controls everything you do, learn, think and feel. It also makes sense of everything around you.

Your brain has two sides. The left side is in charge of the right side of your body, while the right side is in charge of the left side. Different parts of the brain do different jobs.

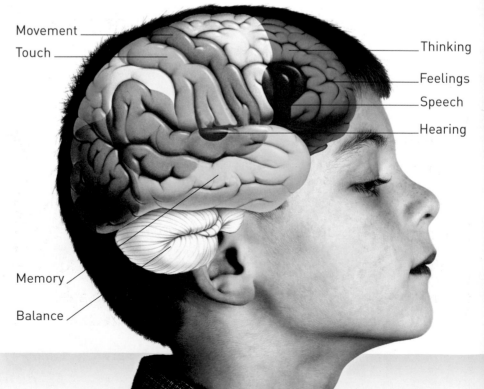

Movement

Touch

Thinking

Feelings

Speech

Hearing

Memory

Balance

Nerves

Spinal cord

Your brain is connected to the rest of your body by **nerves**, which are like long, thin wires. From your brain, the nerves travel down your back, in a thick bundle called your spinal cord. Then they branch out in all directions.

Nerves carry messages to and from your brain. The messages are in the form of electrical signals and they whizz around inside you at high speed.

Funny bone

Have you ever bashed your elbow and felt a strong, tingling pain? Ouch! That's because you have hit a large nerve that lies close to the surface. People often say they have bumped their 'funny bone' when they hit this nerve, even though it is not a bone at all.

Seeing and hearing

Seeing and hearing are two of your five **senses**. You see with your eyes and hear with your ears.

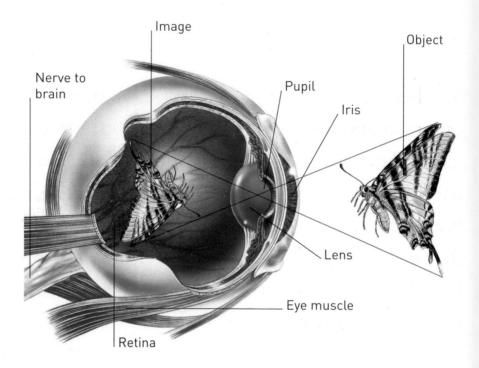

Image

Object

Nerve to brain

Pupil

Iris

Lens

Eye muscle

Retina

You see things when light bounces off objects and goes into your eye through the **pupil**. The lens focuses the light on the **retina** at the back of your eye, where it makes an upside-down image of what you are seeing. Nerves send this image to your brain. Your brain sorts the image out, makes sense of it and turns it the right way up.

Sound travels deep inside your ears.

You hear things when sounds travel into your outer ear and down a long tube, called the ear canal. They hit a piece of thin skin, called the ear drum, and make it vibrate, or wobble. Tiny bones pick up these vibrations and send them deeper inside your ear, where there is watery liquid. As the liquid wobbles, it pulls on nerves that send messages to your brain.

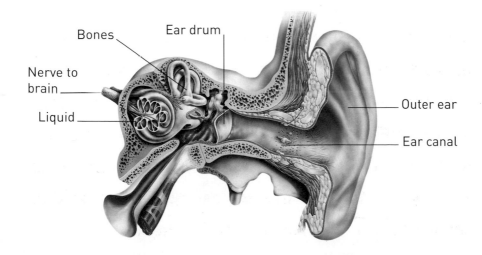

Bones

Ear drum

Nerve to brain

Liquid

Outer ear

Ear canal

Tasting, smelling and touching

Tasting, smelling and touching are your other three senses. You taste with your tongue, you smell with your nose and you touch with your skin.

Your tongue is covered in tiny bumps, called taste buds, which pick up different flavours and send messages about them to your brain.

Taste buds

Your tongue helps you to taste sweet, salty, sour and bitter things. What does an ice cream taste like?

You smell things with your nose. When you breathe in, smells travel up your nostrils and are picked up by nerves inside your nose.

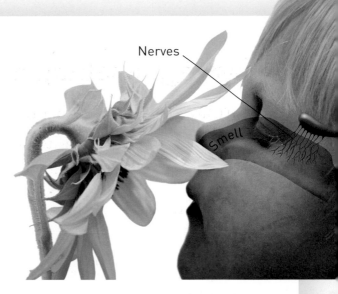

Nerves

Smell

There are millions of tiny nerves packed into your skin. They help you to touch and feel things. They tell your brain if things are hot, cold, sharp, hard or soft.

Most sensitive

Your most sensitive skin is on your fingertips, lips and toes. They have the most nerve cells. The skin on your back and bottom is the least sensitive.

Lungs

Your body needs a gas called oxygen to live and grow. Oxygen helps your body to release energy from the food you eat. You breathe in oxygen from the air through your nose or mouth. The air goes in through your nose or mouth, down your **windpipe** and into your lungs. In your lungs, the oxygen passes into your blood and is carried around your body.

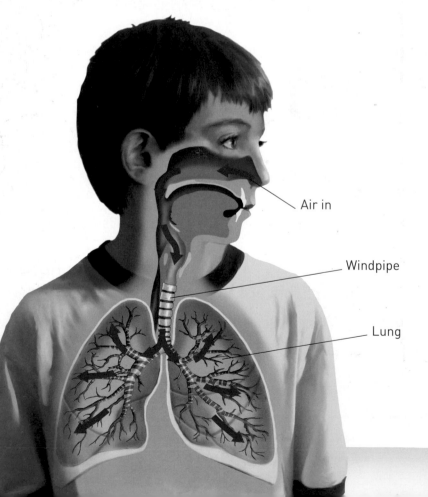

Air in

Windpipe

Lung

As your body uses up oxygen, it makes a waste gas, called carbon dioxide. This passes from your blood into your lungs and then out of your body from your lungs when you breathe out.

You breathe harder when you exercise to get more oxygen to your muscles.

Breathing

When you breathe in, your chest muscles lift your ribs up and out. Your chest gets bigger, so your lungs have space to fill up with fresh air. When you breathe out, your ribs move in and down, which squeezes used air out of your lungs and out through your nose or mouth.

Heart and blood

Press your hand on your chest. Can you feel your heart beating? Your heart is a very special muscle, about the size of your clenched fist. Every time it beats, it pumps blood around your body. Your heart beats between 80 and 100 times a minute.

This is what happens every time your heart beats.

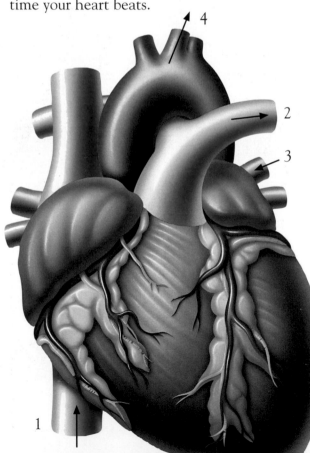

1. Blood needing oxygen flows from your body into your heart.

2. It is pumped to your lungs to pick up a fresh supply of oxygen.

3. Fresh blood from your lungs flows into your heart.

4. It is pumped to the rest of your body.

Blood flows around your body in tiny tubes, called **blood vessels**. Its main job is to carry oxygen from the air you breathe and goodness from the food you eat to every part of you.

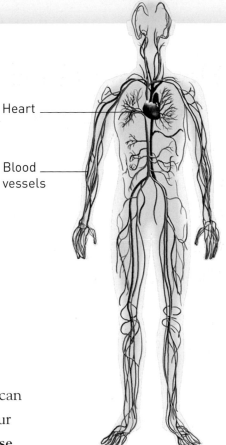

Heart

Blood vessels

By pressing on your wrist, a doctor can feel the blood pumping through your body. This is called taking your **pulse**.

Stomach and digestion

Your body needs food to work properly. But first, food has to be broken down into tiny pieces so that your blood can carry it around your body. **Digestion** starts when you take a bite of food.

Teeth

Your first teeth are called milk teeth. From about the age of six, these teeth start to fall out and your adult teeth push through. You have 20 milk teeth and 32 adult teeth.

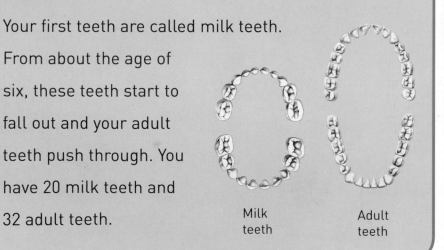

Milk teeth

Adult teeth

1. In your mouth, your teeth chop and chew food. **Saliva** makes it slippery and easy to swallow.

2. Food is squeezed down a long tube, called the **oesophagus**, into your stomach.

3. In your stomach, food is mixed with digestive juices and turns into a thick, slimy soup. Then it goes down another long tube, called the small intestine.

4. In the small intestine, more juices mix with the food. The useful parts of the food pass through the thin walls of the small intestine into your blood and are carried around your body.

5. Waste food goes into the large intestine. Then it passes out of your body when you go to the toilet.

Liver and kidneys

Blood carrying digested food travels from your intestines to your liver. The liver takes out any poisons (toxins) and makes the food safe. It also takes some of the goodness from the food and stores it until your body needs it.

Your liver is criss-crossed with blood vessels, carrying blood to and from your body.

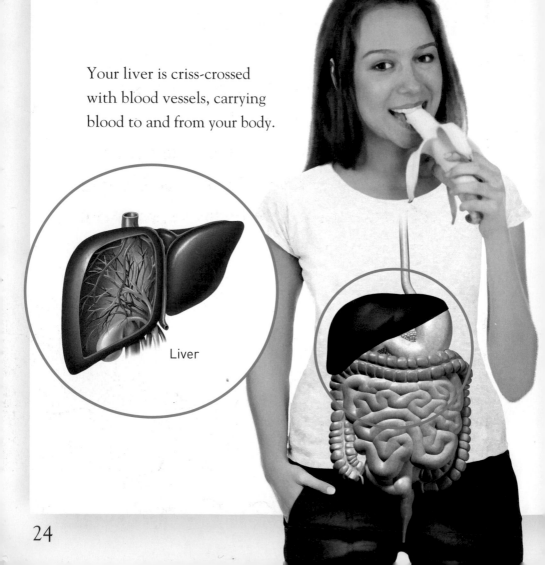

Liver

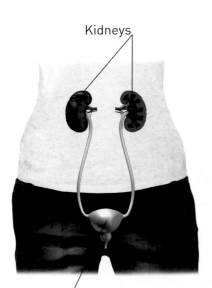

Kidneys

Bladder

You have two, bean-shaped kidneys in your lower back. They clean your blood and take out waste that could harm your body. They also get rid of any extra water that your body does not need.

The waste and extra water makes a liquid called **urine**. It flows down two tubes into a stretchy bag, called your **bladder**. When your bladder is full, you go to the toilet and the urine passes out of your body.

Drinking

You can drink about two mugfuls of liquid before your bladder becomes full and you have to go to the toilet.

Birth and growth

Your body is amazing but how did you begin? You started life inside your mother's **womb**. You grew in your mother's womb for about nine months until you were ready to be born.

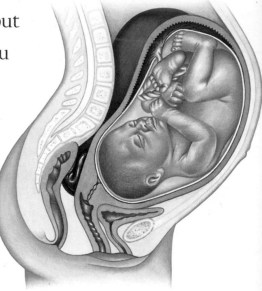

You turned upside down to be born.

After you were born, you had to be fed and carried when you were a baby. As you got older, your body grew bigger and stronger. You learned lots of new skills, such as walking and talking. You were able to do more things for yourself.

A baby crawls, then learns to walk.

Your body will carry on growing until you are about 20 years old. You grew very fast for the first two years, then more slowly. You may have another growth spurt when you are about ten. Your body will keep on changing as you grow and get older.

Illness and health

If something goes wrong with your body, you become ill. Many illnesses happen because tiny living things called germs, such as **bacteria** and **viruses**, get inside your body. This is how you catch a cold, for example.

Your body fights the harmful germs and kills them. Sometimes it does this on its own, but a doctor may give you medicine to help. When you were a baby, you had lots of **vaccinations** to help your body fight off germs. A vaccination is a small dose of germs that stops you getting a disease.

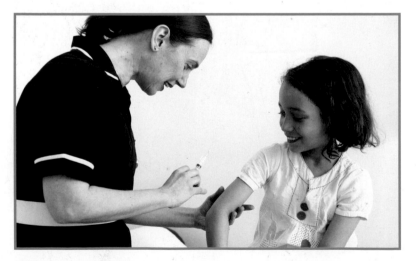

This nurse is giving a child a vaccination.

Staying healthy

You can do lots of things to stay healthy. You can eat different kinds of food, with lots of fruit and vegetables, and exercise to keep your body fit and strong. Make sure that you get plenty of sleep and keep your teeth and body clean. Clean, healthy bodies can fight off germs and diseases more easily.

Glossary

bacteria Tiny living things, some of them harmful, that are everywhere, including the human body.

bladder A muscular bag that fills up with urine until you can go to the toilet.

blood vessels The tubes that run all over your body and carry blood.

cells The tiny units that make up every part of your body.

digest To break up food into tiny pieces so your blood can carry it around your body.

digestion The process of breaking down food.

germs Tiny living things that can cause illnesses.

joints Places where two or more bones meet and allow you to move.

nerves Cells like long, thin wires that carry messages between your body and brain.

oesophagus A tube that carries food from your mouth into your stomach.

pulse A regular throbbing in your wrist or neck caused by blood being pumped around your body.

pupil The hole in the middle of your eye through which light enters.

retina The area at the back of your eye that has lots of sensitive nerve cells.

saliva A liquid in your mouth that helps to swallow food and starts to break it down.

senses Seeing, hearing, tasting, smelling and touching are all senses.

tendons Strong bands that attach your muscles to your bones.

urine A waste liquid made by your body.

vaccinations Injections that protect you from some types of illnesses.

virus A tiny living thing, even smaller than bacteria, which causes some diseases.

windpipe A tube that carries air into and out of your lungs. It is also called the trachea.

womb The part of a mother's body in which babies grow until they are born.

Index

babies 26, 28
bladder 25, 30
blood 5, 11, 18, 20, 21, 23, 24, 25, 30
bones 4, 6–7, 8, 15
brain 6, 12, 14, 15, 16, 17
breathing 18–19

cells 5, 10, 11, 30

digestion 9, 22, 23, 30

ears 8, 15
exercise 19, 29
eyes 14, 31

fingerprints 11
food 18, 21, 22, 23, 24, 29

germs 10, 28, 30

hair 4, 5, 10, 11
heart 4, 6, 9, 20

joints 7, 30

liver 24
lungs 4, 6, 18–19, 20

muscles 8–9, 19, 20

nerves 13, 14, 15, 17, 30

oxygen 18, 19, 20, 21

ribs 6, 7, 19

senses 14–17, 31
skin 4, 9, 10–11, 17
sweat 10, 11

teeth 22, 29
tendons 8, 31
tongue 16

urine 25, 31

vaccinations 28, 31

waste 19, 23, 25

X-rays 6